The 5Cs
of Successful
Women

Paula Sugawara

The 5Cs of Successful Women

Copyright © 2020 by Paula Sugawara

All rights reserved.

Table of Contents

Acknowledgements

My first big thank you has to go to all the amazing women I have worked with during my own career and as an executive coach. You were the inspiration behind this book and seeing how you have been able to make your own paths to success inspired me to share those stories and my own research with others.

I would also like to thank Elizabeth Okada and Tanja Bach for their input and support when reviewing my manuscript – their feedback, comments and frank suggestions were immensely invaluable. Thank you to friends, acquaintances and connections who, when they heard I was writing a book, continued to encourage me – their passion and excitement was a major source of motivation

I am also extremely grateful to the women who shared their personal stories for this book – taking time out of their busy schedules to contribute. I love that each story is different and we have edited to a minimum so that readers can enjoy the wide range of experiences these women share.

Lastly to my mum, Avril Smith, for giving me some many chances in life and always being my cheerleader and my children, Hugo and Romy, for being with me and there for me. Thank you.

Author Bio

Paula was born in Halifax, UK and after graduating from the University of Nottingham, and working in Spain, moved to Japan where she has spent 32 years of her life. Her first "work" was a modern day version of the nativity story she wrote for school assembly at the age of 13 and had always wanted to write a book. Her career was mainly in investment banking followed by talent development and she currently works independently as an executive coach and facilitator. She is a strong positive thinker and believer in people. "Women in leadership" is a theme close to her heart and she has used her experience working with women in a wide range of industries and at various levels to show other women how they too can succeed in their life. This book was produced solely by women, from the author, to beta readers, editorial, book cover design and formatting.

For more details on her, please refer to her website

www.tokyoconsultingservices.com

Introduction

This book is intended to be a combination of learning and action. Structured in two parts, the first half details the 5Cs with practical tips and reflection exercises. The second half is a compilation of personal stories from successful women sharing their journey and learnings, hopefully to provide the reader with a source of inspiration.

After sixteen years of coaching male and female clients, from a variety of nationalities, cultures and in a wide range of organizations and roles, I realized that the women I coached could be divided into two groups: Those who are highly successful and those who are not reaching their full potential.

To clarify, there are already many women in relatively senior roles who have stagnated in their career; therefore lacking the progression they could still achieve. There are also a lot of women who don't have the same aspirations and haven't really thought about expanding beyond their current role. However, it is important to remember that there ARE opportunities for women to get further up the career ladder. There ARE ways for women to expand beyond what they are currently doing. It also doesn't mean that all women must be leaders or on the board of directors; nor that women need to be ambitious and want to climb the career ladder. There are a lot of women, however, who are not getting the support in their career that they deserve or reaching their full potential.

Although it is perceived that there is a glass ceiling for women in many organizations, there is also another clear reason behind that lack of advancement: women. They are the ones who are often limiting themselves with their own mindset, and by changing their approach, they could take advantage of many more opportunities.

This book aims to provide women with the tools and strategies to do this, and those women who are seeking to move beyond where they are right now – whether that is to the top of the corporate ladder or an expanded role at current levels. This does not exclude women who are happy at their current level but may want more recognition or responsibility in their current position.

My aim is to encourage women to think about why they are not getting what they want from their careers and lives, and how they can start to reflect on this. I'd also like to encourage them to think about where they'd like to be and how to take the necessary steps to make it happen. I recommend a simple framework—The 5 Cs—to help make those changes.

Chapter One
Courage

What is courage? Isn`t confidence more important?

Courage and confidence go hand in hand, and both are equally important. In saying that, courage comes first because without it you would have difficulty getting to the confidence stage. Courage helps you take that first step, whereas confidence comes from doing something repeatedly and becoming more adept.

Courage is the secret ingredient which allows you to act despite your fears. We need courage to give us that little push to begin something, allowing us the ability to put aside the fear of failure and take the first steps. It helps us to create a virtuous cycle, leading to increased confidence.

We often see courageous people as those who are not afraid, but that is not necessarily the case. They are probably just as afraid as anybody else - the difference is that they don't let fear hold them back. They address it head on and use that fear to drive them. It is also important to remember that it is OK to be afraid. Fear is not a bad thing, so embrace it and use it to your advantage.

The Courage Cycle

Identify Your Fears

Take Action

Create Success

Build Confidence

Creating the Courage Cycle

Identify your fears

The concept of fear of the unknown is quite well understood. Embracing fear and making the effort to understand what your fears actually are is very important in reducing them. The first step in this process is naming the fears we have. Is it the fear that the project won't be successful? Or fear that you won't be able to answer questions in a meeting? It is important to identify the fear you are experiencing, as essentially, not understanding what we are afraid of stops us from moving forward.

In a business context, when coaching clients who are being hampered by their fears, I have found it useful to further explore what the root of their anxiety is. Questions such as, "If this project fails, what is the worst thing that might happen? Will you be fired? Will you be demoted? Will your salary or bonus be cut?" Usually the answer is none of these. Once people comprehend exactly what the consequences are, the fear they feel is likely to subside very quickly.

Take action

Once we realize that the downside is not as scary as we had thought, it is important to take that first step as soon as possible, before those fears re-emerge. Those first actions should be baby steps, so that we can establish the foundations for building confidence. Questions such as, "If X happens, what will you do?" "If you don't get the promotion you are hoping for, what is the next step?" Even if the only response you have is to cry, that alone can be considered a step forward as it acknowledges your emotions, and therefore allows you to move on afterwards.

Create Success

Taking action in small steps helps to build up a bank of successes. If the first steps are too big, they appear daunting, and we are likely to not be as motivated to take them. Find an easy step you can take, and take it. Remember to look back on these events, to remind yourself of what you have achieved. This, in turn, fuels confidence going forward. For example, if you find giving presentations with confidence is your challenge, maybe try some of the mini milestones as below:

- Create your own elevator pitch (maximum 90 seconds)

- Record a recent presentation you have made, and find two things you did well and two things you can improve on

- Ask a colleague to listen to a five minute snippet of a larger presentation you have done, and ask them for feedback

- Practice the beginning and end of your presentation

- Look for the opportunity to make a presentation to your team or colleagues so that you can increase your confidence for larger forums

Build Confidence

As we create success, keeping those wins at the forefront of our minds, allows us to remember what we can do, rather than what we can't. Reminding ourselves of all the things we have achieved, spurs us on to do more. How can we create those courageous moments which will lead us to build confidence?

Let's have a look at some opportunities where we can show courage in the workplace using The Courage Cycle.

Showing courage in the workplace.

1. Actively participate in meetings.

How many women do you see attending meetings, who are not actually taking part? Meetings are for people to share opinions, discuss, listen and be heard. Unfortunately, many participants are often held back by the fear of not having the right answer or being of an opinion that is different to others or not deemed to be the "acceptable" one. Taking that first step to playing a greater role in meetings requires a lot of courage and useful steps to take are:

- Commit to asking at least one question during a meeting

- Look for opportunities to build on someone's existing comments

- Try and comment on a discussion which is outside of your usual area of expertise

2. Take action:

a. Share ideas.

How often do we hold back from sharing our ideas? And why do we do that? If the reason you are holding back is the fear of not having the right opinion, being 'incorrect', or later being proved to be wrong, what action can you take? Giving yourself a quick reality check could be helpful. Who said opinions need to always be 'correct', or that only fully formed and perfected ideas should be shared? Nobody. So, don't let this hold you back. If your ideas aren't 100% complete, using statements such as the ones listed below can help get them across:

"I`m still working on this idea, but so far, I`m thinking..."

"I haven't finalized my ideas on this yet, so I'm looking forward to your input."

"I'm still going through the brainstorming process but..."

Using these statements will signal to the audience that your ideas are not yet whole and give you the option to revise them or even discard them at a future date. Remember, it is OK to have an idea that is still a work in progress, and not every idea or opinion has to be correct. In the end, it's better to be wrong, than to not have a voice at all.

b. Ask questions

Don't be afraid to ask questions in order to find out more and check your understanding. Again, it's about having the courage to accept that you don't have all the answers and are comfortable admitting that. Look for opportunities to summarize what has been said and play it back to check your understanding. Play devil's advocate – asking those important "what if" questions to again further your understanding.

For example, what if you continue to take the same approach as in the past? What would the impact be on your future?

c. *Give Feedback*

Delivering constructive feedback also requires courage. It's easy to avoid giving feedback due to not wanting to hurt a person's feelings, demotivate them, or being afraid of their reaction. However, please remember that feedback is a gift. It gives the receiver the opportunity to change an undesired behaviour or learn from a mistake they have made. The majority of people in organizations are usually appreciative of feedback, so again, it is something we should be actively looking to do.

It is also easy to say, "I'm not a manager, I don't have any direct reports, so there's nobody to give feedback to." However, feedback can be given to your peers and people who don't report to you with the positive intent of helping overall. By creating an environment where people are free to give feedback at all levels, you will be building a more positive atmosphere, which leads to improvements in all directions.

There are many feedback models that can be used as part of a constructive conversation, an example of which is below.

4R Feedback Model

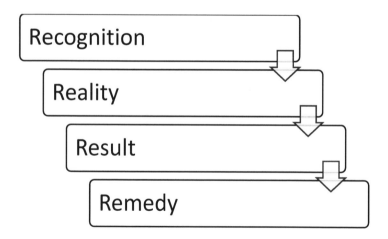

This is a four-step conversation on how to deliver emotion-free, constructive feedback.

Recognition

Feedback should only be focusing on one specific behaviour or action. Not everything that person does is wrong, or needs fixing. Start off the conversation with something positive that you appreciate about them.

John, I see you've been working really hard on Project C recently. Your effort is really helping us to make this project successful and I appreciate your input.
Thank you for that.

Reality

Developmental feedback should always be based on facts and reality; actions you have seen and can prove if necessary. Second hand accounts and rumours are not acceptable. Ensure you have all the facts you need and don't start your sentence with 'but', as this will only negate the positive comments you made in the recognition stage!

*Today, I'd like to talk to you about
something I've noticed recently – your
lateness. You were late twice this week and
once last week.*

Result

Many people do not realise the impact of their behaviour or just haven't thought that far ahead. An effective feedback conversation can provide them the opportunity to consider the potential adverse effects of their actions and reinforce the need to improve or change.

*John, when you are late for the office, how
do you think it might affect those who work
closely with you – or even our clients?*

Remedy

There are two approaches to helping somebody find a remedy for their negative actions.

Coaching approach – encourage the employee to find their own solution. By working this out for themselves, there is a better chance that they will commit to the new change. This creates accountability and a higher probability of behaviour improvement.

So I'd like to hear how you think we can resolve this situation and how I can best support you?

How do you think you can avoid being late in future?

In this situation, John might suggest taking an earlier train, getting somebody else to take his dog for a walk in the morning or not staying at the office so late the previous evening. The manager may not have been able to suggest these ideas, due to the personal nature of the solutions.

Directive Approach - There are some situations where the manager may want to be clear about what behavioural changes he or she wants and what approach they the person should take – i.e. the directive approach. An example of this is:

I realize that commuting can be a challenge, but I'd like you to make a big effort to get to

the office 15 minutes earlier than usual,
then if things do go wrong, you won't be
late. If there are times when you think you
ARE going to be late, then please make sure
to call ahead and let us know what time you
expect to arrive.

If you note in the 4R model, the conversation we have shown in the example is very much free of emotion, with no blame and no complaints. It merely points out a behaviour, why it has to change and what the options are going forward. Since there is no emotion involved, it makes it easy to deliver this kind of message and reduces the likelihood that it will escalate into a heated exchange.

3. Ask for Feedback

In addition to giving feedback, women should take every opportunity to receive it. It is, unfortunately, fairly common knowledge that women regularly get less feedback than their male colleagues. Asking your manager, peers and even direct reports for regular feedback is another important way of showing courage in the workplace.

4. Don't accept it

Another aspect of showing courage and speaking up is pointing out something that is not acceptable and looking for the opportunity to be the voice of others. If you see a policy that is not acceptable, maybe even discriminatory, by not speaking up you are allowing it to continue. Courage requires telling the truth and taking the opportunity to lead by example.

Putting it into Practice

1. Identify two or three meetings where you can actively take part. Prepare your comments in advance so that you are ready to participate and share your views.

2. Identify occasions where you may need to share your opinions or ideas, and have a couple of ideas prepared with explanations, in an easy to understand format.

3. Identify opportunities to give both positive and constructive feedback to a colleague. Use any of the recognised feedback models that remove the emotion from the discussion and keep the conversation on track.

Chapter Two
Confidence

Why is it that, on a global basis, women now outnumber men in terms of both university attendance and graduation (56% of college degrees in the US are gained by women, for example) however once they join the workplace, this position starts to change. Consequently, we see women start to lag in terms of employment, income, and business ownership.

Research shows that one of the greatest factors holding women back is confidence. In 2011, the Institute of Leadership and Management, in the United Kingdom, surveyed British managers about how confident they feel in their professions. Half of the female respondents reported self-doubt about their job performance and careers, compared with less than a third of male respondents. Essentially, men tend to overestimate their intelligence and academic abilities, while women tend to do the opposite. Yet, the quality of performance between men and women is statistically around the same. A classic example of this mindset is applying for a new job or promotion. Men will often look at the ten skills required for the role, decide they have seven of them and apply. Women will look at the same list, decide they also have seven skills, but feel that it is not enough, so they don't apply.

Women are frequently told they need to be more confident, but what does being confident really mean? Essentially, it is a combination of a can-do attitude that is part mindset and part success track.

As an executive coach, I am often astounded at senior women telling me they don't feel confident or are suffering from 'imposter syndrome'. If they are not feeling confident, then what hope is there for the rest of us?

Dealing with Imposter Syndrome

Described as a mixture of anxiety and a persistent inability to recognize one's own success, Imposter Syndrome can have a major impact on career progress. Originally identified in 1978 by psychologists Pauline Clane and Suzanne Innes, it was originally thought that imposter syndrome only affected women; however it has since been proven to also affect men. Further research has shown that women tend to suffer from imposter syndrome more adversely though, as they produce less testosterone, which has been identified as the confidence hormone.

So how does imposter syndrome affect women? Research by NatWest (UK banking group), as part of its #OwnYourImposter campaign, revealed some very disturbing data.

- 60% of women who have considered starting a business chose not to proceed due to lack of confidence

- 28% of working women feel like imposter syndrome has stopped them speaking in a meeting

- 21% have been prevented from suggesting a new or alternative idea at work

- 26% have failed to change career or role

Self-talk

How does imposter syndrome show up in working women?

"You don't know what you are doing."

"Any moment someone will catch you out."

"What made you think you could even attempt this."

"You're a failure."

"You're not good enough."

That little voice in your ear? This is our self-talk. This voice is often not what others might say to us. Because we hear it in our heads, and it's what we are telling ourselves, we tend to believe it.

Once we have identified self-talk, and know the kind of messages it sends us, what do we need to do? Switch it off!

How do we switch off negative self-talk?

1. Remind yourself that you are in this position or role for a reason and you were selected because of your skills or your experience. Your manager believes you are the best person for this job.

2. Remember all the successes you have had in the past and the great achievements you have made. Make a list of them and read it regularly.

3. Ask yourself, do you seriously believe you are less worthy or qualified for this role than some of your male peers? Do you believe you are less intelligent than any of your male peers? No. I thought so. Remember this.

4. Recall the feedback you get from your peers and direct reports. They mean the positive things they say, so you better believe it!

5. Remind yourself that you are an important role model and other women are looking up to you, wanting you to succeed. Your success will inspire others.

6. You don't need to win at everything. It's ok to make mistakes, to not be perfect, to not have all the answers. Being comfortable with that will help you build more confidence.

7. Don't compare yourself to others. You are you. Not anybody else. You don't need to prove yourself to others – or yourself. Embrace the whole package that is you!

8. Find your power outfit. Look through your wardrobe for that one outfit or item of clothing that helps you to feel confident and powerful. Confidence is not just about appearance, but we can often get a boost

from a special pair of shoes or jewellery. That kind of investment is worth it.

9. Practice your power pose – Wonder Woman! There is a lot of proof behind the psychology that standing in a power pose for a couple of minutes before an important event or appearance can help to build confidence. Research shows that higher levels of the hormone testosterone (in both men and women) lead to increased feelings of confidence, while lower levels of cortisol lead to decreased anxiety and an improved ability to deal with stress. Levels of both hormones can vary depending on the social, physical, and environmental cues around you. One of the physical cues is body language.

Tests carried out by Harvard University identified a range of high power (open and relaxed posture) and low power poses (closed and guarded posture) and measured the hormone levels during each stance.

The results showed that by adopting high power posture and striking a variety of power poses testosterone levels increased by 20% whilst the cortisol levels reduced by 25%. How can you replicate this? Adopt the Wonder Woman pose for two minutes at the start of every day – chest out, hands on hips, legs slightly apart. This will gradually help you feel more confident, even if that is the opposite of what you're actually feeling. Faking it till you make it is an important part of confidence building.

How can women display confidence at work?

Now we have switched off the negative self-talk, what else can women do to show more confidence at work? What are the habits they need to establish and the approaches they can take?

Be Selective

If you get the opportunity to choose which projects to work on, try to align your workload and objectives with those of your boss and the organization. It is often tempting to choose the easy or more enjoyable projects to work on, but by becoming a proactive strategic contributor, you become an invaluable asset to your team and to the organization. By adding value in this way, you will be increasingly appreciated, and this will help to build confidence.

Be Strategic

Showing your strategic skills and approaching projects with that same mindset can give you the time to build up to success and foster confidence.

- Look for opportunities to think 'big picture' rather than focusing on the short term or what is close at hand

- Find ways to add value. How can you improve a process, make something more efficient or cut costs?

- Question the status quo – what can we do differently? What needs to change?

- Listen. Listen. Listen. Actively searching out and listening to the opinions of others can help to create new perspectives and generate new ideas

- Think outside the box. Starting with 'crazy' ideas and gradually funnelling down to something more realistic is a great way of generating innovative approaches

- Surround yourself with strategic thinkers. Taking the opportunity to bounce your ideas off other strategic thinkers can help fuel your own thought process and approaches.

- Become an impact thinker – what is the impact of this decision or action?

- Challenge yourself – what am I not doing? What might I have missed?

Adopt the Progress Principle

Created by Harvard Business School researcher, Teresa Amabile, her study of 12,000 workday accounts showed that the most important thing leading to a sense of positivity, is celebrating small wins. Tracking progress and noting those little wins helps to create feelings of productivity, engagement and even happiness.

Ask yourself questions such as:

- What went well today?

- Where did I add value?

- How did this win make me feel?

Applying this approach to your list of accomplishments each day, and seeing your own progress in larger tasks, will reinforce the fact that you are contributing to the organization and help to boost confidence. This record can be kept as a reminder of why you are valuable and how you have contributed when it gets to your end of year review and salary talks!

Manage your visibility

You can display confidence by looking for opportunities to be more visible within the organization. As mentioned in the courage section, establishing your presence in meetings is vital if you want to appear confident. It is important not to stay quiet. Planning how you can contribute, making statements of agreement or volunteering for projects are all great places to start.

Be decisive

Women can often tend to be the diplomats in an organization, making sure everybody is on board with decisions. However, there are only so many times that you can ask the opinions of your colleagues and get everybody's buy in on decisions. These are the times when you have to thank people for their input but move forward with the next steps. Ensure you are taking charge and making decisions when needed. As you do more of this you will find it creates a positive cycle of confidence. One additional approach to making decisions is to use a rational decision-making model such as the one below – knowing you have gone through all the necessary steps required, will fuel confidence in that final decision.

Rational Decision Making Model

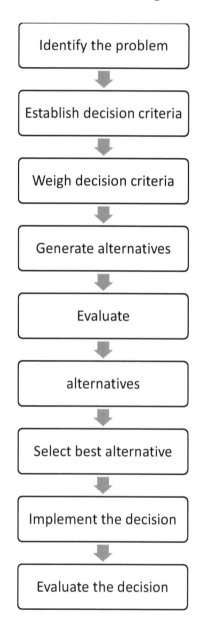

Identify the problem

Establish decision criteria

Weigh decision criteria

Generate alternatives

Evaluate

alternatives

Select best alternative

Implement the decision

Evaluate the decision

Confident Body Language

In addition to the power pose we already discussed, there are many aspects of body language that women need to be aware of. Here are some important tips to bear in mind:

- Make eye contact – Although there are cultural nuances about maintaining eye contact, in the western business world, looking people in the eye indicates trustworthiness and openness, as well as confidence

- Lower your vocal pitch – High pitched voices can be considered less emphatic and powerful

- Be aware of nodding too much - Women often want to show agreement and understanding and habitually nod too much. This can be distracting and can also be taken as a sign of somebody who readily agrees to things.

- Use open gestures – Keep movements relaxed, using open arm and hand gestures

- Talk with your hands – This helps to keep your hands occupied (avoiding the dead-man pose!) as well as emphasizing key points and keeping the audience interested

- Smile – It's important to smile but make sure it is genuine. Women have been trained to smile and nod when talking. However, fake smiling can be seen as both a sign of weakness and falseness. Use your smile only when appropriate, then it will be appreciated more.

- Be aware of nervous gestures - Fiddling is a prime demonstration of nerves. It's not uncommon to see women touching their hair or fiddling with jewellery, but the actions are considered low confidence gestures and should be avoided. If you catch yourself doing them, try and steady yourself by placing your hands on the desk or table, or your feet flat on the floor to 'ground' yourself.

- Avoid adopting an overconfident demeanour - Having thought about how to look confident and generate the feeling from within, it is also important that we don't go too far. It is not uncommon to see women overcompensate when they try to appear confident. I call this 'testosterone mode', when they decide that they must show more of the male aspects of confidence. I see many examples of women who then become monster managers, not willing to listen to those around them, and barking orders and directives all day long.

Putting it into Practice

1. When you are in a situation and you feel you are lacking in confidence, ask yourself, why am I feeling like this? What are the thoughts that are going through my head? Are those judgements I am making about myself true?

2. Make a list of all your past achievements and successes. Refer to this on a regular basis.

3. Ask your friends and family, what do you like, respect, or appreciate about me? What are my strengths? What do you see me doing well?

4. Set yourself small goals in terms of participating in meetings. Prepare your thoughts and comments in advance, and make a conscious decision to take part at least once in your next meeting. As you start to grow in confidence, increase the frequency of participation.

Chapter Three
Communication

Top Three Communication Strengths
–Female and Male

Female	Male
1. Ability to read body language and nonverbal cues.	1. Physical presence.
2. Good listening skills.	2. Direct and to-the-point interactions
3. Effective display of empathy.	3. Body language signals of power

Top Three Communication Weaknesses – Female
and Male

Female	Male
1. Overly emotional.	1. Overly blunt and direct.
2. Meandering - won't get to the point.	2. Insensitive to audience reactions
3. Not authoritative.	3. Too confident in own opinion

Carol Kinsey Gorman Ph.D -The Silent Language of Leaders

Unsurprisingly, men and women communicate differently in the workplace. Women may have the edge in collaborative environments (where listening skills, inclusive of body language and empathy, are more highly valued), and men are typically believed to take charge more readily and be viewed as more effective in environments where decisiveness is critical. It is these differences and communication challenges which can often hold women back.

What are some of the communication challenges that women need to be aware of?

1. *Reflect on how you speak*

In reality, effective communication is not about trying to confuse people, nor is it about trying to appear clever by using a lot of big words or data. It's about choosing the most accurate and appropriate words and being clear, brief and to the point. Have you ever sat through a meeting or presentation where the speaker talks too much and takes forever to get to the point? What is the impact it might have had on you?

To avoid the impression of having a meandering communication style, it pays to be prepared beforehand when making comments. It is important to know the key message you want to get across in advance. By focusing on the ultimate goal of the conversation, you'll be less likely to veer off topic. Thinking before you speak helps you rein in the rhetoric that others often hear as rambling or excessive. Honing in on a precise purpose will enable you to get your message across clearly, whether you're in an interview, on the phone, or in a team meeting.

2. *Structure your comments*

Adding structure to your comments can make them easier to express and simpler for the listener to understand.

- Try using techniques such as bullet points and using numbered references. For example, 'there are three key factors…'

- Begin your comments with a conclusion. "This is what I think, and here are the reasons why."

That way, there is a greater chance that people will listen to you without switching off before you get to the end of your points

3. *Adding a qualifier*

A good idea would be adding a tagline so comments don't sound too aggressive, without diluting your message. For example, consider this headline: "We must change our marketing strategy by the fourth quarter of the year or we will lose a significant market share. I say this for three reasons: First, we haven't changed our strategy in over five years and the market has changed significantly in that time; second, our products have changed and require a different approach to marketing; and third, buyer preferences have changed and we have not addressed those preferences." Listen to how a tagline used at the end changes the tenor: "You can tell that I feel strongly about this. I'd like to know what you think so that we can get the best ideas on the table to move forward." A few extra words and exhibiting interest in what others think, helps to diminish the impression of stridency..

4. Be concise.

Women, in an attempt to soften the delivery of a strong message, unconsciously use more words than a situation calls for. As a result, their messages and intent are diluted (often to the point of being indecipherable).When answering a question or making a comment, do just that. No need to repeat it, no need to add context. Just share your points and shut up! A good approach to use is KISS – Keep It Simple and Short

5.   *Get comfortable with difficult conversations.*

In their book, *Asserting Yourself: A Practical Guide for Positive Change*, Sharon and Gordon Bower provide a simple technique—DESCript Method—for confronting others in a way that allows you to express yourself, while maintaining strong relationships. This is particularly helpful for women who have the need to please others and therefore avoid conversations to circumvent a confrontation. To begin a difficult conversation, I recommend these four steps:

1. Describe why you want to talk.

2. Explain your viewpoint and elicit the other person's.

3. Specify desired outcomes.

4. Clarify consequences (positive or negative).

When listening to the other person, agreement is not necessary. Simply an acknowledgment that they've been heard is sufficient. You could say, "Joe, I'd like to talk to you about something that happened in the meeting this morning. Each time I tried to make a point, I was interrupted by you. It made me feel as though what I was saying wasn't as important as what you wanted to say. Did you realise you were doing this?" Pause to listen to what they say, and then follow up with, "I hear what you're saying. What would be helpful is if you would fully hear me out. I promise to do the same for you. This way, we can mutually build on our strengths."

6. *Clarify expectations rather than just saying no.*

If you want me to complete the review by lunch time, please be aware that won't give me time to check as thoroughly as I would normally like to. If you are ok with this, I can go ahead however, if you can give me some more time, I feel confident I can do a more thorough job. Which would you prefer?

7.   Write well

Writing gives you the opportunity to consider what you want to say with greater care and structure it before expressing your thoughts. It enables you to get your ideas out on the table and be articulate about your position, persuading people of your argument clearly and in a compelling way. Don't forget to proofread your emails; not just for spelling and grammar but for the tone and emotional element. Emails can sound very brusque and demanding and get people's backs up, so be careful of sending them out when you are feeling irritated or angry.

8.   Be direct AND nice

Many women are reluctant to ask for what they want/need for fear of being seen as too demanding. As a result, they disguise their requests in flowery language making it unclear as to exactly what they are wanting. Conversely, they go to the opposite end of the spectrum and become overly assertive in their requests, resulting in appearing aggressive. Don't be afraid to ask for what you want/need but remember it's important to find that right balance of being direct but also being nice.

9.   *Ask for feedback*

How can women ask for and receive more feedback? Who do they ask? Research shows that on average women receive significantly less constructive feedback than men. It also shows that the feedback received can often be vaguer and less direct. According to the Women in the Workplace 2016 report by Lean In and McKinsey, women are 20% less likely than men to get feedback which could help them to improve their performance. Reasoning behind this is generally the fear of how women might react (the bias that they will react emotionally) or any constructive feedback could be taken negatively and adversely impact the relationship. As a result, it is important that women actively reach out to request feedback. If you are told that you are doing a great job, then ask, specifically what you are doing well. If you feel that the feedback is vague, ask for specific examples of that behaviour.

10. Logic vs. Emotion

It is important to make sure that your discussions in the workplace are based on the appropriate mix of logic and emotion. We often try to isolate decisions to make sure they are purely based on reason and fact, but doing that can overlook the emotional part of our gut instinct. In most persuasive situations, people react based on emotion, then justify their reactions with logic and fact. A message that is based largely on emotion will often act as a warning to logical thinkers.

"Has she thought this through?"

"What is the logic behind this decision?"

In contrast, a logical message which doesn't appeal to a person's emotions will often fall flat, failing to elicit the desired response. Therefore, we need to make sure that any discussions combine both elements.

11. Use assertive language

Often, by trying to be polite and not wanting to say no, responses come across as being non-assertive. The other side of that is when women then use aggressive phraseology to reinforce their position. The table below gives some examples of the range of communication styles from non-assertive to assertive to aggressive. Think about the kinds of things you might be saying and rephrase them into assertive forms.

Non-Assertive	Assertive	Aggressive
I'm not sure if it would be possible, but do you think you could let me have that information when you get a minute?	Please let me have the information we discussed in time for my meeting tomorrow at 10AM	Give me that information by 10AM tomorrow without fail

Is it at all possible for me to leave early tonight?	I am leaving at 4pm and will make sure I come in early tomorrow to make sure we are able to meet the deadline	It's not my fault we are busy. I have to leave at 4pm.
I'm very busy and working to a tight deadline but I might be able to help you for a short time	I won't be able to do it by the time you asked, but I will do my best to get you something by 11AM.	No way can I get it done that quickly. That's impossible.

12. Keep business correspondence professional

Unfortunately, there is still a tendency in some cultures for women to communicate in a 'cute' way so that they don't appear too aggressive. However, emails with lots of exclamation marks, emoticons and abbreviations etc. make them appear nothing less than incredibly unprofessional and can severely damage credibility. Instead of using the 'cute' card, it's important to aim for a commanding voice, unafraid to show intelligence and suggesting commitment to the job. Gaining respect is done through hard work and a clear dedication to the task at hand, and not via appeasing everybody and unnecessarily apologizing or dumbing yourself down.

Putting it into Practice

1. Prepare your comments for an upcoming presentation or meeting using the DESCript model.

2. Review how you communicate verbally – look for opportunities to replace emotional phrases and wordings with logical and assertive ones.

3. Ask your manager for two or three examples of feedback – constructive and positive.

4. Review some of your most recent email messages - Is there an opportunity for these

to be rewritten in a less emotional and more assertive way?

Chapter Four
Connections

How Women Network

Despite the fact that a wide range of data shows the importance of networking, women tend not to network as much or as effectively as they could or should.

First, it is important to remember that women will tend to network differently as circumstances often prevent us from taking the same approach as men. Many women are unable to attend events after work due to family commitments, and avoid networking with men in social settings in order to prevent any situations that might be misconstrued.

Another noteworthy point is that women who might try to network in the same way that men do might not see the same level of success. According to a 2019 study by the Kellogg School of Management, this is because they would then be missing out on a close inner circle of women. The study showed the importance of a tight-knit female group for the critical information on job opportunities and the challenges it can provide. Specifically, 77% of the highest achieving women in the study had strong ties with an inner circle of two or three other women. Those who form a strong inner circle with other women who can share career advice, are nearly three times more likely to get a better job than women who don't have that same support system.

How do women specifically network differently?

1. Whereas men often focus on the short-term need and develop wide and potentially loosely connected networks, women tend to

build longer term personal connections or friendships.

2. Even with those relationships that women succeed in establishing, they are often reluctant to leverage them. Women tend to hesitate in asking for support and can feel moral concerns about using their network – especially if they feel that they can't return the favour equally. This, unfortunately, results in missing chances to establish important connections and the upside of those connections.

3. When women seek a mentor, they tend to look for someone they would like to be friends with, rather than someone they can learn from. As a result, they often don't get the feedback they need to get ahead. Meanwhile, men look to form alliances and are often willing to do business with somebody they might not even like, if it will help them achieve their final goal of success. This is because they have an implicit

understanding that this relationship can be dissolved when it is no longer convenient, as might not be the case with a long-term friendship.

Savvy Networking

1. Ask for help and recommendations

It's no secret that networking is the key to getting selected for stretch assignments that often lead to promotions, meaning it's completely acceptable to ask for help in this area. Especially when you know the guy in the office will be asking for support in this area. Women have significantly less access to, or interaction with senior leaders, so having somebody in your corner is beneficial. Those interoffice connections can assist them through company politics, recommend them for stretch opportunities or advocate for their promotion.

2. Get strategic

Do not confuse friendship with mentorship, however. When you are networking, try to be strategic. Stakeholder mapping (see the explanation below) is an excellent exercise for you to take a step back to look at your network; who is in it, who needs to be in it and how to forge important relationships.

Stakeholder Mapping

1. Draw a small circle with your own initials inside it, on a large piece of paper.

2. Think of six to eight important relationships – those you can approach for career advice, sponsorship, a sounding board or to challenge you. It's also worth including those who can have an impact on your career – they might be part of the selection committee for promotions, leading a department you are interested in moving to, or just generally senior people in the organisation.

3. Make a basic assessment of each relationship in terms of strength. Five is a very strong relationship – one is very weak.

4. Connect these people to each other if there is a connection. The lines should range from dotted lines for fairly weak connections to single lines, then to double lines for more tangible connections.

5. This should give you a visual representation of the current relationships you have, which are important, and which need to be strengthened. It will also give you a clearer idea of the interconnecting relationships and if you can use person A to connect you to person B and so on.

6. Creating a strategic relationship can take time and is definitely not something which happens overnight. Start on this as soon as possible, to enable you to get those relationships in place and gain the vital support from those who will be your cheerleaders.

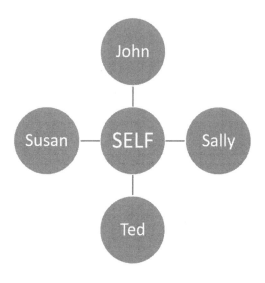

3. Get yourself a mentor

If you don't have a natural mentor you can call on within your organisation, then an alternative approach is to ask for one to be assigned to you. More and more companies are starting to support internal mentorship programs, where they assign mentors to promising employees. This ensures that there is a recognised process that can be followed and gives mentors guidance on how they might be able to support their mentees as effectively as possible. Extraordinary mentors provide you with 'real life' insights into the dynamics of power and politics; audacious mentors are top-level executives who push for your promotion to the top. Essentially, a strong mentor relationship will be led by the mentee, reaching out proactively to drive the relationship.

Linking into LinkedIn

Although it would never replace face to face, "real life" networking, LinkedIn is a great way to connect with people who it might be difficult to connect with directly in other ways. It's important to make sure that your own profile is up to date and inspiring. For example, no old photos or out of date job experience. Your LinkedIn profile is a perfect opportunity to showcase your skills and experience to potential recruiters, clients, vendors etc. and should not be underestimated.

Spread your networking tentacles far and wide

Although inside your organization is often the best first step to build your network, it is important to also look outside your company. Professional networking events are a great source of connections, but we often forget other sources. These can include previous academic relationships (alumni associations and university friends), friends and acquaintances, parents of our children's friends, neighbours, people we know via the local gym etc. These are all potentially great sources of connections and we shouldn't hesitate to ask for introductions and try to expand our network.

You don't need to be friends with everybody

It has already been well documented that women often spend a lot of time in the workplace, trying to be nice to everybody – even to the extent that they put their own needs last. Although it is recommended to get on with colleagues, it is not necessary to be best friends with everybody in the office. Women often feel that they should be friends with other women – out of a sense of female sisterhood or loyalty. However, men are not necessarily as concerned if they felt there was a personality clash. There will always be people who you are never going to gel with. Let them go.

Putting It into Practice

1. Make a start on your stakeholder map. List a minimum of 6 connections, based on the instructions above.

2. Formulate a plan on how to strengthen the weaker relationships you have identified. Who can connect or introduce you to others on that map? How can you get some face time with those people you already know but would like to know in more depth? How can you get exposure to the senior people you may need to know?

3. Make a list of the other potential sources of networking. Aim to list at least 10 relationships you can establish via connections outside your company

4. Virtual networking – do you have a LinkedIn profile? Is it up to date? Set yourself a weekly target of connections you want to make via LinkedIn and start searching for the right people on there.

Chapter Five
Career Path

According to research by Catalyst, in 2019, 29% of senior management roles are held by women, the highest number ever on record. In addition, 87% of global businesses had at least one woman in a senior management role in 2019; encouraging data compared to previous years. Bearing in mind however, that approximately 47% of the workforce in the US is women, and only 4% of S&P 500 companies have a female CEO, there is still a very long way to go. Sadly, what often holds women back is the female mindset, and part of this is from not having a career plan or path in mind.

Last year, during a pilot program to introduce the concept of this book, I asked a group of sixteen women at a major international truck and bus manufacturer, what their career goal was. Out of that group, only three answered with a specific goal, such as, "I'd like to get a promotion", "I'd like to be a manager", "I'm keen to work overseas" etc. Other replies ranged from, "I don't really have a goal" to, "I'd like to be the go-to person regarding XYZ" or, "I'd like people to think they can come and ask me anything".

We cannot complain about lack of career opportunities if we have not considered our own career goals or paths for the future. Having a career path doesn't mean that you want to be the next CEO of your company. Without an idea of where you would like to go, it is very difficult to start on that route or to get the help and support you will need.

Women don't ask for career support

According to the KPMG Women's Leadership Study of 2019, 69% of the women surveyed did not feel confident about asking for a career path plan. The same trend is shown when requesting a promotion (65% do not feel confident), or asking for a raise (61%), or a new role or position (56%). During my coaching career, when working with very senior women, we often discussed their being uncomfortable with having these vital career conversations. But you can bet your bottom dollar that the guy in the next office is not holding back and is making sure his career path is clear and on track.

Why the lack of comfort? Women often feel that asking for a promotion or discussing their career path is pushy or too assertive. My counsel is to be proactive and start a conversation with your manager, along the lines of:

"What are the career options you see for me?"

"What would be a potential career path for me?

"Where might I see my career go over the next three to five years?"

These are all perfectly valid discussions to be having. If we consider the number of programs that some of the world's largest organisations have for women, it is fair to assume that companies want women to succeed. However, if women don't know what they want, then all the support in the world is not going to get them there.

Adopting a Self-Promoting Attitude

In addition to the one on one discussion with managers, it is important to also self-promote so that people in the organisation are aware of what they want from their careers, and more importantly what they can expect them to contribute. By self-promoting, we don't mean boasting. It is about stating your position and highlighting your strengths and abilities. It is important to adopt language that explains the impact you believe your work is having on your clients, customers, or community. Also, women need to own the mentality of, "I want to be here, I want to build my career here, so I will give this job my all." Sharing this mentality with your peers will enable you to maximize on opportunities that come your way.

Avoiding the blame culture

"The company doesn't give me chances", "I would never get promoted", are widely spoken, but often we are not taking those chances or looking for them. It's not wrong to want a career or advancement within an organisation. Nor is it wrong to want to keep your career low-key, if you have family circumstances you need to prioritise, or if you prefer to be in a support role instead of a front line one. What is wrong is wanting opportunities but not reaching out for them.

According to a 2014 internal report by Hewlett-Packard, men will apply for a job promotion if they feel they meet 60% of the criteria, while women will doubt their credentials unless they meet 100% of the qualifications. The solution? Apply anyway!

Instead of thinking about missing qualifications as a weakness, adopt the mentality that this is an opportunity to sell your determination to succeed. Don't be afraid to promote yourself. Consider framing employment gaps as opportunities to capitalize on your previous experience. Think of how you might have experience from other areas or skills you can adapt. It is very rare for an employer to be able to hire somebody who has all the skills required for a specific role, so if you are worried about how to explain gaps at the interview then be prepared with a road map of how you could get these skills and experiences once you have started on the role – like in the First 90 Days approach (First 90 Days: Critical Success Strategies for New Leaders at All Levels by Michael Watkins).

Get qualified

We often think that qualifications stop with university or graduate school. Of course, these are necessary but in effect are nothing more than an entry point for a career. It's unlikely you would get a white-collar role without some kind of degree or specialist college qualification, but often the kind of degree you have is largely irrelevant. What is often overlooked is the wide range of specialist qualifications that can be taken at a later date and don't require a four-year university course. When thinking of a career move or looking at a possible step up within your current organisation, it is worth considering the qualifications which might help you along that path. In addition to the wide range of online courses and distance learning, there are often short-term courses which require three or four day's participation in classroom training. There are also combinations of both options – online learning, supplemented by a set number of days spent in the classroom. As you investigate these opportunities, it is also worth discussing internally with the human resources or Learning and Development team as they may be willing to subsidize or even fund the whole program.

Duties of a job evolve, and employees need to evolve too. While you should always play to your strengths and core competencies, expanding your skill set doesn't necessarily have to mean signing up for a course. It can also include reading a book or other self-study, mastering a skill that you might be weak in or attending a conference on a new theme or emerging industry. The up-to-date knowledge you gain from these would be further increased by the important connections you make, enabling you to further expand your network. Bottom line — the more well-rounded you are, the better.

Develop your team

When considering the next career move or promotion, it is quite common to see women focusing on the I – what they want and how they can achieve it. However, if you overlook the WE, it's going to make that move difficult. Imagine how frustrating it would be, to be in the remaining few candidates being considered for a promotion, when the conversation turns to succession planning. "If we promote her, who will take over her current role?" There are many examples where a leader is ready for promotion, but their team is not, because there is no logical or appropriate successor. So, while looking above for that next promotion, it is vital to also look down and see who below you is ready to take that next step too which would fill the shoes that you leave empty. You might be ready, but are they?

Take a long-term career view

When we think of a promotion, we often look at what the next step might be this year or next. It's worth taking a step back, however, and thinking on a larger scale. Where do you want to be in five years, or even ten? That kind of long-term view gives you the opportunity to be strategic and start planning – to build on the relationships you need, get experience in some of the areas where you have gaps, gain skills that are missing and connecting with decision makers. Putting your hand up for one off or short-term projects can help you to expand your range of experience. Volunteering on internal committees can help you further expand your network and potentially increase exposure to senior management. Taking the lead on specific initiatives can give you a chance to practice leadership before taking the step up to management. When it becomes time to take that next step, we can then refer to the experiences we have already gained using concrete examples. In contrast, by only focusing on gaining the next promotion, we tend to think about how to get that role without actually considering if we have all the necessary pieces of experience and the appropriate skill set. This can then be met with disappointment upon finding out that we don't have the skill set we thought we had.

But what about kids?

Admittedly, the childbearing role of women can have an impact on careers. Taking time off – whether it is a very short maternity leave, or a longer childcare leave, will impact our careers. But also, we need to take this in perspective. If we assume that the average person's working life is around 40 years then taking off 1-2 years, or even more, to give birth and take care of our children is small in the grand scheme of things.

Speaking from experience, it is definitely not easy juggling kids and a career, but it is definitely do-able, and more so in the current climate, where working from home is commonly accepted.

Putting It into Practice

1. Review your career plans – do you have career objectives for the next two to five years?

2. Set up a time to discuss with your manager what some of your career options might be.

References

Chapter 3 Communication

Carol Kinsey Goman, Ph.D., 2011 "The Silent Language of Leaders: How Body Language Can Help - or Hurt How You Lead"

Personal Stories

Kathy Matsui
Vice Chair
Goldman Sachs Japan

During the course of my 30-year career in finance, I've made many mistakes and learned multiple lessons about navigating one's career and managing others. Here are three pieces of advice that have helped me along the way.

Worst advice.

I'll start with the worst advice I was ever given. It was 'Work hard, keep your head down and someday someone will notice you and you'll get promoted.' While it's obviously important to work hard and do your best, I've come to realize that it doesn't really matter if no one notices. I learned that not only do you need to excel at what you do, but it's also important to keep one's antennae up, build one's network, be aware of opportunities, and make sure that you're visible to senior leaders. There is no 'invisible hand' that magically lifts you to a promotion, so you need to be conscious of where you stand within the organization, and what concrete steps are required to get you to where you want to go. If you don't know any of this, you need to ask.

Work-life balance —> Work-life equilibrium. After returning to work from first maternity leave, I was filled with stress, I was striving for 'work-life balance,' which I interpreted to mean that every day, I had to be: 1/3 perfect mother, 1/3 perfect career woman, and 1/3 perfect wife. But when I was at work, I felt guilty not being with my new-born son (and calling home every hour to check if he was breathing!), and when I was at home, I felt guilty that I was neglecting my work commitments. After several months of guilt-ridden stress, I had an epiphany. I decided that striving for a perfect equilibrium was futile, and that it was better to aim for a 'work-life equilibrium,' where every day, I'd just do my best in whatever I was doing, and stop

71

feeling guilty about not accepting every late-night conference call, and feeding my kids fast-food meals. Everyone - men and women- has a different equilibrium every day, and over the years, I've discovered that perfection is not only impossible, but it's also meaningless.

Personal BOD

Formal mentorship relationships are helpful, but in my experience, I've found that during the course of my life, I've needed to lean on different people for advice, and one of my colleagues recommended me to create a 'Personal Board of Directors.' For instance, when I was starting out, I needed senior people in my firm to help me navigate my career. When I became a new mother, I desperately needed help from experienced mothers. When I was diagnosed with breast cancer, I needed support from cancer survivors to get me through the psychological challenges of my illness. The members of my BOD have become my trusted advisors, and while I don't need advice from all of them all the time, I know I can lean on them when I need help, and they know they can count on me for the same.

Kathleen Hurd
Corporate Coach and Facilitator

When I thought about how to approach writing this piece, I really struggled with where to start. What could I say in just 500 words that would have an impact? 500 words seem like nowhere near ENOUGH.

See, I've spent most of my life being a perfectionist with a love of diving into the details, but the thought of "just 500 words" reminds me of what I've learned about the importance of keeping things simple.

Often in life we work things up in our brains to be far more complicated or time consuming than they need to be. In my current job as a personal development coach, I've learned so much about how focusing on simplicity can help us to build momentum and make progress more quickly than if we get hung up on all the details in a state of analysis paralysis.

For example, I started thinking about how to move towards self-employment when I had a 5-month old, a broken foot and a husband that was MIA for 3 weeks due to mandatory training in Europe for a new job. My company was downsizing and had presented me with an offer to leave, but I had failed to get into any of the public day-care in our neighbourhood and in a fit of overwhelm turned down the offer and exercised my right to an extended childcare leave. I read a book on coaching and knew it was the perfect fit, but then stagnated for three months, my brain insisting that I needed more information, to be more prepared. I knew what I wanted to do, literally the only thing holding me back was choosing and paying for a coaching course.

I was plagued with thoughts. What if I choose the wrong one? Should I pick the $3000 one or the $10,000 one? Should I study in Japanese or English? But all the English classes are late at night...and how much time should I invest? When can I even start working? What's the point if we don't get day-care? And if the perfect alternative job comes up right after I pay, what then?

None of these thoughts were helpful to me in making progress and I am so very glad when one day in June 2019 I heard back that a class exactly fit my criteria and would be starting the next evening. I ripped off the Band-Aid and went for it. Was it the best coaching course I could have chosen? No. Did it matter? No. Because it got me DOING THE WORK and taking steps to focus on doing what I wanted to do rather than being hung up on all the things that weren't that important.

Now I run my own business. My husband and I spend lots of quality time with our son. We travel when we want to. I meet interesting people and help them to figure out what they want for their lives. I am so glad that I went for it so I could get to this place in my life.

This can apply anywhere in your life. Next time you feel like you are struggling, I urge you to think of how to keep it simple, focus on the big picture, and then take that next step.

Laura Sheehan

Owner & Principal Strategist
E.P. Career Strategies

Success is a word, a concept with which I struggled greatly. Only when I realized that success was a matter of choice was I able to truly come into my own.

I began my professional journey as a U.S. lawyer. In this very traditional role, I envisioned my career path as one that would allow me to scale the corporate ladder over time, making measured progress and receiving regular recognition for my accomplishments along the way.

Equally important to my career, however, was the notion of having a life partner and children. When I married, my husband's job almost immediately took us overseas. As law and advocacy seemed to be in global demand, I was sure I could find opportunities to work anywhere my husband's job might take us.

Over the span of nearly 20 years, we lived in eight countries. We had two children along the way. Though from the outset I had known that our life would be one of regular transition, I had not fully realized the challenges inherent in maintaining a "traditional" career whilst constantly on the move. I found work in each location, yet most of the positions were only tangentially related to my background in law. Having not lived up to the original vision I had for my career and life, I grew sad, angry and very resentful. I felt an utter failure.

The turning point came when I was nearly 40. A milestone year, prompting a mid-life review and self-evaluation. As chance would have it, the timing coincided with another international move.

Having just arrived in our new host city, I was preparing to begin the job search once more. I was invited to attend a newcomers' lunch where

Fortune assigned me to a table of women - all of whom were expat parents who worked full-time outside of the home. One a diplomat, one a teacher, one a tech professional. When it came time for me to answer the (somewhat dreaded) question, "What do you do?"

I provided the accomplished group with a list of laments over a lost career in law, a fate I felt forced to accept as a trailing spouse. In response, one of the women paused, and then pointedly asked, "If you could do anything, what would it be?"

And with that one query, a world of possibilities again opened up. I could CHOOSE to do ANYTHING!

No longer locked into the limiting belief that I needed to continue to pursue a traditional career in law, my perspective immediately shifted from all that I thought I had lost...to the true wealth of knowledge and experiences I had gained. I could clearly see how all of the pieces of my past fit together and that each was not a stumbling block, but a strong foundation I had slowly built over time.

In that pivotal moment, I realized that if I could do anything, it would be to help others overcome (or altogether avoid) the many challenges I had in being an accompanying partner and expat on the move. I immediately announced my intention to become a career coach and strategist. Five years later, I have an established consultancy and have served hundreds of clients worldwide. When asked what I do, I now confidently, joyfully state, "I help people find their place, wherever they are - in life and in the world."

Anonymous

Regional Account Manager
Global Services Company

I must emphasize the importance of clear career strategy and communication especially for successful women compared to men. I hate to make anything about gender politics; however there are assumptions for different genders. This is not about what you feel, it is about a community culture, a company culture, a society/country culture, and all of those combined. Even a very progressive company may be influenced (often subconsciously) by the society around them.

If you have no strategy for yourself, you may fall victim to those assumptions without even being aware of it. In a way that may not happen to your male counterparts regarding their careers and positions in the company. The onus, therefore, is on us as women to be more aware and conscious of our career goals and anything short of clarity on the goals must be supplemented with communication.

Also, as one of these assumptions is related to family and child rearing, we also need to be clear to our partners, friends and colleagues what that means to US, not what it means to the company, the community or the country.

In my personal experience, after having my second maternity leave, I was ready to discuss my return to work. I was preparing to ramp up and kick butt. I am a salesperson, and this means putting in the time and hitting the pavement, as they say. I was preparing to take my sales career to another level and my full potential. I was taken aback when my manager presented an agreement that was a similar level in the business with a lower salary. Thankfully, I knew to assess the background and ask questions before saying what I was really feeling. Through discussion, we discovered that the manager had imagined me spending more time at home and envisioned my career leaning into my past successes and pulling away from the grind of a sales floor. I had to correct that assumption before I could negotiate a better package.

If I did not ask the questions, I would not have understood the background and I would've easily assumed this was discrimination. In reality, it was just community assumptions at play and an attractive and supportive offer for someone taking a different career path: one more balanced with home life. The same tips could be applied to any career man wishing to work in a different way than the company, community or country typical imagine.

Communication is key. Clear strategy is also critical. If someone helps to make your career for you and lay the path, you are in a unique position. We make it happen with a clear vision and strategy to realize it then communicate, communicate, communicate.

Paula Sugawara

Melanie Brock

CEO, Melanie Brock Advisory
Founder, Celebrating Women in Japan

Our definition of success has probably changed since the coronavirus pandemic began. Mine has. The pandemic has given many of us reason to reconsider our approach and to think carefully about what is important to us. Sadly, for many, this change will have been forced as a result of health or economic reasons, with the future of work, study pathways and employment, of significant concern. Perhaps our worlds will ultimately be determined from a pre or post 2020 viewpoint.

In an 'after corona' workplace, whether it is online or office-based, or indeed a hybrid version of the two, what won't change is the importance of community. Community will continue to hold us true and to support us. It is an extension of ourselves and our beliefs. Maybe 'community' can be the 6th "C" added to what are all important factors of success: courage, confidence, communication, connections, and career. Community.

My sense of community developed early on as a product of life in a small town and a family committed to belonging, be it through Mum and Dad's shops or Rotary (Dad was a lifer!), our schools, not-for-profit groups or sporting organisations, teams my sister and brother and I supported and barracked for.

Japan was added to that community in 1982, when I lived in Aomori for a year as an exchange student. My network broadened to include Japanese host-families and my sailor-suited fellow high-school friends. Add to that university, part-time jobs, fellow mums I met in hospital when having my sons, parents and teachers at day-care and school. A community of colleagues and team members from the various jobs and roles I have had, chamber of commerce community, those also involved and passionate about Australia-Japan relations, Tohoku and the amazing network of women in the #CelebratingWomeninJapan project.

Living in Japan, creating a life and a home here, but also staying close to my 'home' in Australia and family has been tough. Absolutely thrilling at times too. Working in another language and not always knowing what is going on behind the scenes (this happens a lot) makes for many disasters and triumphs. A truckload of mistakes and frustration. I cringe to think of the pain and grief some of my cross-cultural clangers have caused over the past 38 years!

When things have been tough and everything seemed too difficult, someone from some part of my amazing community would lend a hand and help me get through things. That was no more evident than when I arrived in Tokyo with my two young sons in tow, for six months! in 1995. 25 years later, a longer stay than we had planned, I remain ever grateful to the community of 'day-care mums' and teachers at primary school.

Being a single mother in any country is tricky but being a single mum in Japan is very hard work and I owe my sanity to the day-care mums and teachers who set me straight and supported me. Single mothers are subject to a stigma, tougher financial circumstances and so much pressure from society. Too much pressure.

I know the extra pressure placed on single parents, particularly mums, from coronavirus, has added to this. A recent survey [by the Single Parent Support Association] indicated that nearly 70 percent of single-parent families have reported an income drop during the coronavirus pandemic. With 75 percent of those respondents being single mothers, it's great to see activities like that of the Hitori Janai Project, which have compiled NPOs that support single parents, particularly mothers, across Japan. It's incredibly important to know you're not alone as a single parent.

I suspect that while I had a stock of resilience from how I was brought up, a load more resilience landed in my lap from being a single mum. Having the community of day-care mums, some of them single mothers and single fathers themselves, gave me strength and the will to keep on fighting the good fight. My resolve was fortified thanks to this community. As was my liver. Many a glass of wine was had discussing how to tackle something and just letting our kids be together.

My heart goes out to single mums in this pandemic. We need to work harder to create a society that supports the most vulnerable in our midst and not further stigmatise them. That is the opportunity open to us now. It is up to us to ensure the success of others by building a more flexible and tolerant workplace and society. One that gives equal opportunity and a voice to single mums and single dads as well as those in more traditional families.

Early on in my career, I received some very pointed advice about the value of a community or network. That advice called on me to learn the importance of networking for the sake of building a community, and not just amassing contacts or business cards, as some tend to see it today. That old friend reminded me how important it was to be genuine, authentic, and generous with your community. That people can see right through a pretender and that faking it was a sure-fire way to fail. He also reminded me that any attempt to quickly capitalise on these connections was best avoided - that you had to be in something for the long game in Japan and to stay true to your community. This strikes me as important advice for us all, at all stages of our careers.

While I continue to live through disasters and triumphs, I know that it is the power of my community that keeps me going. Hold on tight to your own community and value the lessons and love it shows you in return. There is nothing better!

The Leap of Faith
– From Lifeshakes to Lifequakes.

Karen Faehndrich
CEO Australia
Audrey Page & Associates

Nine years ago, I was the APAC CEO for a global institution in the Workforce Transformation space when we were acquired by our largest competitor. During the weeks that followed, I was interviewed and offered the opportunity to be the CEO Asia for the integrated business. This offer came with a non-negotiable requirement to be based in HK.

Whilst I had been travelling the world and the APAC region endlessly in my previous role, I had never been an expatriate. This was a daunting, heart-breaking, and exciting proposition all at once. For me this was a lifeshake!

I took the leap, packed up and left everything I loved behind. This was a time of significant change, personal insight, professional development, and surprising moments. I took absolute delight in the good, the bad and sometimes the downright ugly.

To survive the road ahead, the amalgamation of two big global brands across the Asia region, I needed to take a huge leap of faith and hang onto an unshakable sense of confidence to ride the waves.

I adopted the philosophy of playing the long game, staying focused on the ultimate objective. I learnt quickly that you could hold opposing ideas without necessarily having to reconcile them and the value of choosing several good solutions to a problem, experimenting with them all, with the best way forward rising naturally to the surface in clear sight of all.

Leading with kindness and positive intent, particularly during times of difficulty and when colleagues are experiencing elevated levels of discomfort, helped to shore up alignment and a collective vision.

Managing possibility against a backdrop of strategic intent, even in the face of great ambiguity, takes a delicate balance of creativity, composure, and the ability to take multiple perspectives into consideration.

It is fair to say that I had great success in shaping the strategic direction and growth of the integrated business. My approach had been deliberate and tenacious with an unwavering commitment to excellence, innovation with insight, business enhancement, stakeholder engagement and the attraction of the best talent l could afford in support of my efforts.

I attribute key characteristics that I have focused on and paid attention to as the foundation for my career advancement, fulfilment, and success. They also shape how I show up for both myself and my team every day, they are:

- Trust and humility

- Building emotional and intellectual agility

- Navigating the political landscape

- Choosing my battles and the timing

- Establishing meaningful relationships and sponsorship

- Listening to connect

- Living to learn

- Leading authentically

- Curious enthusiasm

- Focusing on change that matters

- Recognising greatness in others

- Taking joy in success

- Taking wisdom from failures

- Community - Never go it alone

Eighteen months ago, my decision to return to Australia to join Audrey Page as CEO Australia was also a deliberate one. I brought with me a clear vision to reset and elevate the agenda, reimagine the idea of transition pathways and all underpinned by the notion of lifelong learning to shape careers and fuel inclusive economic growth.

And so, my new journey began, pursuing my vision, fulfilling a commitment to creating value, mobilising a community of leaders, and advancing the idea that fluid circumstances require flexibility.

With the recent COVID pandemic, life, and work as we know it has abruptly changed and the level of ambiguity for many brought an overwhelming sense of disorientation. This has not been easy for me as the sense of being exiled from my normal boundaries has heightened frustrations which swell and subside with a greater or lesser intensity. Realising this recently, I knew it was time to take some breaths and acknowledge that this time of great disruption for me is best described as a lifequake.

In this knowledge, I made a commitment to using this time as a unique opportunity to connect with the core of who I am, a 'meaning-making exercise' and unique opportunity to gain insight and wisdom.

I was reading 'For Life is in The Transitions' by Feiler and stumbled upon a series of steps to help bring my day and week into positive focus:

- Accepting the situation

- Marking the change

- Shedding old ways

- Creating new outlets

- Sharing my transformation

- Unveiling my new self

- Telling my story

- Expressing gratitude

In addition, I focus on meaning, which is enduring as opposed to happiness, which can be fleeting. Meaning brings the past, present and future into focus and is larger than the self. I took great solace from this advice.

It is important to always remember, jobs will come and go but careers are personal, ownable and expandable.

Our journeys will be different, but we also know that lessons shared galvanise us, so we don't turn away but instead, lean in with fierce determination. I hope this very brief glimpse into my story does just that for you.

Dian Mertani

Formerly of IBM Japan

I was a young employee in my second year of career in a huge IT company in Japan when I learned that I was expecting my first child. Normally in Japan, this is a clear pause for any women`s career. In this modern yet conservative and traditional country, women are culturally expected to slow down, take at least two years off. Many women choose not to come back for years to the workforce; let alone thinking to climb the career ladder.

Working from home, in Japan at that time, for a woman, was nowhere in the picture. But I refused to follow it. Career and parenting can go side by side. I came from Indonesia where most pregnant women start maternity leave just days before the due date so they can spend more time on maternity leave i.e. 15 weeks allowance with the baby after birth.

When I returned to work, I used the "advantage" of being a foreigner, nothing to lose, not knowing much Japanese language (so it saved me from knowing too much of the negative sayings). Having my own mind and international exposure, I just broke the ceiling.

I set up a meeting and made a professional pitch to my management. I presented my proposal to work from home after the baby was born. I approached it like a project proposal, listing down the background including WHO recommendation of breastfeeding, why I need to be with my baby instead of dropping her at day-care. What the company can expect from me in terms of my target and performance. How the decision related to the company's culture to support work balance and women. I tackled all the questions and answered the arguments. All in a professional manner.

Management finally approved it. I was perhaps the first woman allowed to work from home for maternity in the company and believe I paved the road for other women. After weeks of maternity leave, I continued to work and handled my work projects from home while caring for my new-born until seven months old. My career moved forward without pause.

Among many career moves and achievement in my 21 years working in corporate Japan, this is one of the things that make me feel most accomplished as a mother, a woman, an employee, and a foreigner. Had I felt hesitant to ask and propose, too scared to break the tradition, too shy to communicate because I was a junior, the story would be different. No matter whether the situation seems impossible, be brave, talk, and ask. It usually gets good results. No regrets.

A story about a pandemic, tourism, and my "C and P"

Gizem Sakamaki
Founder & Owner
Foodie Adventure Japan, Tokyo.

What do you do when your business is in tourism and a global pandemic cancels travel?

Mourning, of course. Falling into a big black hole and mourning the loss of hours of hard work that went into creating and perfecting experiences that turn Japan-travellers into Japan-insiders.

The travel industry was the first thing to go when in February 2020 a Coronavirus epidemic from China, rapidly grew to a global pandemic with high numbers of lives and livelihoods taken in a very short period of time.

Back in March, while the epidemic was still isolated to small parts of Asia, I packed my bags and travelled to Germany to participate in my first large tourism fair, the ITB in Berlin. This was without a doubt going to be the next big step for me personally, and for the career I had built for myself. I had spent weeks designing a pamphlet, picking out contacts to meet, and preparing the tours I would be pitching to possible future partners at the world's largest travel event.

Like many others in Japan, 2020 was going to be MY year!

This story doesn't have a happy ending, does it?

The end of the story is unwritten as the Coronavirus is still unfolding, while scientists race globally to find medical solutions. However, I want to share with you my takeaways from this unfortunate situation, possibly as an example of how to find hope in any kind of personal or professional crisis.

How can a business survive a pandemic, you ask?

Sadly there is no "one size fits all" solution, but I wish to share with you what is keeping me alive and sane in September 2020, six months into the pandemic:

The C and the P

Creativity and Purpose.

I am adding another "C" to the 5 Cs of success, which is Creativity.

While courage, confidence, communication, connections, and career strategy might have all worked well during peace times, I have found deep gratitude for one of my biggest superpowers, creativity, only now, in turmoil. Creativity is what helped me find a solution to a need I saw two years ago and it is what helped me build my business when I was still lacking some of the other Cs, such as confidence, career strategy, or connection.

After many a sleepless night due to financial pressure, as both my husband and I were now self-employed - my brain just wouldn't sit still. It was working day and night to find a solution to the problem at hand: having no work for the foreseeable future.

Having poured time and resources into my tour business for the past two years, I was not willing to turn the lights off just yet, but how could I justify leaving the lights on?

Once again, I let creativity take the lead.

I acknowledged the fact that this crisis was not only a loss, it was also a chance for me to embrace the ideas and skills I had dropped in favour of the tour business; which was more relevant to a growing influx of tourism and the Tokyo 2020 Olympics. It was a chance to start anew, based on my accumulated experience and the help of creativity, courage, confidence, communication, connections, and career strategy.

Having formed many connections throughout my work in tourism, be it as an Airbnb host or as a tour guide, I had a valuable group of followers and supporters to fall back on. I decided to pick up a part-time job on the side that plays into my skills to keep myself afloat for now, while once again honing my creativity to finally work on projects that had been sitting on the backburner for years. Starting from (almost) scratch.

Backburner ideas

We all have them. You have them. I have them. And often only a significant change in our lives pushes us to remember and sometimes even take the chance to realize them.

So I did.

As I mentioned before, my new business ideas are still in the making so this, unfortunately, will be a story with an open ending for now. However, the purpose of this piece is for you to see that creativity is a valuable companion. I believe that creativity and purpose will be the two things keeping me sane and--hopefully someday soon--profitable during this pandemic. You can follow along on this journey through my social media channels and see for yourself which of my back-burner ideas made it to fruition!

I raise my glass to better times ahead

My thoughts go out to all the families and individuals that have been less fortunate than me during this difficult time.

Good luck and health to you, and may this crisis leave us better than it found us.

Yumiko Murakami

Head of Tokyo Centre
OECD

After spending all my adult life outside of Japan, I returned to Tokyo a decade ago from New York. Having grown up in a homogenous environment in Japan, I had thought that I understood the limitations imposed on professional Japanese women and that I was prepared to challenge them. What I was not prepared for, however, was the fact that a lack of diversity was widely prevalent not only for gender, but also for age, nationality, and social/economic backgrounds.

Digitization and globalization have been formidable tsunamis, transforming economies all around the world. Japan is, of course, no exception. In light of a rapidly shrinking population, Japan could benefit greatly from technological revolution such as robotics and automation in order to address severe labour shortages. Globalization could also present Japanese companies with growth opportunities to expand their businesses beyond domestic markets. Yet, the C-suites of Japanese firms are occupied almost exclusively with grey haired Japanese male executives. Where are the young digital pioneers who have never used rotary phones? Where are the foreigners who grew up on cereal and steak instead of rice and fish? And where are the women?

In my view, the most critical part of Japan's challenge is to embrace the diversity of thought. There are indeed companies who proactively recruit women, which is obviously commendable. But are they simply 'checking the box', filling a perceived quota? On a macro economy level, the Japanese female labour market participation rate has been increasing in recent years. While many more women are working today compared to the past, is it truly transformative when female voices are not heard at decision making levels with so few female executives?

Looking back on my college days in Japan some 30 years ago, I recall it was quite an exciting time for young women. At the time, Japanese companies were starting to hire college educated women for professional positions on the back of the newly introduced equal employment opportunity law. I ended up moving to the United States for graduate studies, but I was hoping my college classmates would enjoy wider career options regardless of gender. Fast forward to today, however, you still find very few women are in leadership positions across the economy. These rare female executives have attained their senior positions by working harder than men and assimilating into a male dominated environment. It has implied women had to behave in the same way as their male counterparts if they were to be accepted in the workplace, especially at senior levels.

When women, young people and foreigners sit around the table, they sure look different from older Japanese men. But if their thought processes must comfort prevailing ideas and practices, no one can bring new and innovative ideas to the table. A diversity of thoughts is an essential ingredient for innovation. Much has been talked about how Japanese companies have been striving to become more innovative. Perhaps it is time for them to realize the fastest way to innovate themselves is to embrace different points of views which can be brought to the table by nonconformists.

I would also like to remind younger women in Japan that their value is derived from seeing the world through their own unique perspectives, even if they may differ from those of men. If they try to behave like men, they may lose this edge. Business needs a rich divergence of views, ideas and mindsets to come up with innovative outcomes. Young women are, in a sense, a rare commodity who can command a premium in Japanese business. They should know their voices are extremely valuable and that they should speak up to be heard.

Paula Sugawara

Founder and Executive Coach
Tokyo Consulting Services

For me, a key to my success and being able to advance my career in different directions was another C to add to the list, that of Certifications. Through coaching I have often found that people limit themselves to their qualifications and experience. I don't have experience in X, or I don't have any qualifications in Y – but thinking about "retraining" or getting additional qualifications can lead to several new open doors in our careers. In my case, I found that certifications were able to lead me in a new direction twice in my career, not without challenges, by any means, but certainly with interest.

The first was when I joined the finance industry. For somebody who had a BA in French and Spanish and struggled with maths at school – finance was not a given career move for me. But I found that I loved the buzz of the stock market, learning about different stocks and the companies behind those investment stories and decided that to further my career I should get qualifications. The certified financial analyst (CFA) designation was fairly standard in investment banking, so I signed up for the three-year self-study program – despite the fact that I was still unsure how to calculate percentages! To cut a long story short, I passed the exam and was able to add the CFA designation to my name and use that skill to successfully negotiate a transfer to the research department in Nomura Securities where I had hoped to work for some time.

Later in my career I was able to switch into a totally different direction by gaining coaching qualifications (Professional Certified Coach) which enabled me to start as an executive coach. Again, that was a very new set of skills for me and even with the certification it didn't guarantee being able to create a new career out of it. I started at the very bottom of the coaching tree, by agreeing to coach people for free so that I could get experience in using the various coaching approaches and models I had studied. As my experience grew, I then felt more confident in reaching out to organizations and companies where I had connections to suggest coaching and/or training their managers. Eventually, the combination of these approaches enabled me to build my business and work with senior people in a large range of organizations.

In conclusion, my advice is to use certifications as stepping-stones in your career. Life is long and if you want to it is more than possible to go back to full time education, If you want to retrain in an academic field. However, it is also worth taking a look at some of the online training courses, short term programs, distance learning that are available today to help us polish our skill set and move our career forward or in a different direction. Let's not be held back by our notions that we can only do what we learnt in our youth – we are never too old to learn new things and they can be the key to a successful career.